Beauregard and the Blizzard

wishing you forever friendship
Maureen C. Wacols

For Gabriel
With love from
Aunty Libby and Uncle John
Christmas 2020

Beauregard and the Blizzard

THE TRUE STORY OF A HANDSOME CAT AND THE GIRL WHO LOVED HIM

Maureen O'Rourke Woods

ISBN: 1976597854
ISBN 13: 9781976597855

Author's Note

This story is autobiographical—a true account of the adventure I shared with my cat, Beauregard, at my home just outside Washington, DC, during a treacherous blizzard, now known as the Blizzard of 1966.[1] It was a huge storm called a nor'easter. Of the fifty-nine snowstorms rated on the Northeast Snowfall Impact Scale, it is ranked number thirteen.*[2]

I've named the girl in the story Sara as a tribute to my mother, Sara Stogsdill O'Rourke. In the story my mother is known simply as Mama.

Maureen O'Rourke Woods

*Table 2.

To Mama, who taught me that pets are people.

CHAPTER 1

Sara and Me

It was my most enchanting hidey-hole and the only one I'd never shown my little girl Sara. I'd heard her calling me off and on all morning, but I wasn't ready to go home yet. To you my hiding place would look only like a plain storm-sewer pipe, but from here I stayed wondrously snug and dry while I watched the morning's snowflakes turn the world white, drifting down like long crystalline parachutes, each glimmering with tiny rainbows like the ones Sara always insisted she saw in my lustrous black fur. During the many hours we cuddled and sang purr songs in the sun, she patiently counted out thousands of rainbows.

For her I needed only to count to one—Sara, my one and true best friend. Together she and I were invincible.

It was Sunday, January 30, 1966, and I belonged to a traditional family—Sara; her big sister, Shaun; her little sister, Caroline; Mama; and Daddy. Daddy was an attorney and was gone much of the time. He earned our living, mowed the grass on Saturday, and, upon special request, was available to help us study for tests. Mama did everything else, taking care of our home and everything in it, including us. The spankings so commonly administered in that era never happened in our house. Mama was pretty and fun loving—tough when she had to be but flexible and fair minded, too. But Mama ruled the roost, period. Hers was the ultimate authority, and we did not question it. We adored Mama.

We lived in a redbrick house on a new residential street with a cul-de-sac where we could play. Overall, spending was modest. But in love and respect, I was rich as a sultan, because Mama had taught Sara to treat me just like the other members of our family.

In recent years Caroline Kennedy had shown off her pony on the White House lawn. But Sara was just as proud of me. Besides, Daddy told Sara she could be president herself when she grew up if she studied hard enough. He said a girl's mind was every bit as important as a boy's, but some people didn't understand that. Daddy said sometimes you had to fight for what you believed in. Daddy had landed on D-Day during World War II.

I was given to Sara for her very own when I was just six weeks old, only a bumbling toddler. But I surrendered my soul to her immediately. I was raised in her hands, doing tiny backbends or turning gentle somersaults like a Slinky toy, and in her bed with the pretty red-gingham spread, where I hummed against her neck as she told stories and secrets. She taught me to count on my fingers, pushing gently on each little pad to make my claw come out. "One through ten," she said, "just like on my hands." She said you could add and subtract and multiply, too.

When she patted her hand on the floor, I'd run across the room and rub my head in her palm.

"Look, Mama. Look!" Sara was delighted every single time.

Mama was determined that I'd be raised a gentleman and carefully gave me a gentlemanly name: Beauregard. It was my job to live up to it.

I'd matured inside and out and was now a three-year-old young man in my prime—pure black from head to toe and as shiny as warm glass. I surmised that I was astonishingly handsome—big, strong, sleek, and masculine. Mama insisted that I be neutered as early as the vet would allow. Sara started to object, but Mama said it would keep me from making babies who might wind up homeless. And I wouldn't wander and fight and do something called "spraying," which sounded like something only a ruffian—or an animal—would do. I came home from neutering just the same as I went in, with a little bit less to groom, which was fine with me. I liked to keep myself immaculate.

Sara was still a young girl, only ten as of her birthday just weeks ago. Shaun and Caroline had always been pretty, but Sara wasn't. Her body was slim and strong, but her freckled face was big and round. And her short auburn hair curled in all the wrong places.

"Mama, why am I so ugly?"

Mama just smiled in her confident way and said, "You'll be a late bloomer." That put Sara's mind at ease. Mama knew everything; she must be right.

I didn't care about Sara's face. She was a beautiful companion. Besides, I was good looking enough for both of us.

Oh gosh, there she went, calling me again. She must be close; I could hear her distinctly.

She called my name first and then called "Kitty," going up high and shrill at the end, just like always.

"Beauregaaaarrrrrd! Kitty—Kitty—Kitty—KitEEE? Beau, boy! Beauregaaaarrrrrd! KitEEE—KitEEEE—KitEEEEEEEEEE?"

I felt guilty not answering her, but my hiding place was too delicious to leave just yet.

I planned to come trotting home later; Mama would be thrilled. She always said watching me come home in the snow was a sight to see, a gleaming black boy surrounded by white.

Where was I? Oh yes…

Sara could run as fast and as far as all but the big teenage boys on our street, and she could climb a tree like a monkey. When I was little, I'd scamper up the tree after her and climb just a little higher, too.

"Look, Mama. Look!" she'd call.

But no matter how fast she ran, I could always race past her, now that I was grown. "No fair," she said. "You have four legs, and I only have two." Mostly I just stayed right beside her. It was my favorite place to be anyway.

There were acres and acres of woods behind our house, and we explored them together, especially during the leisurely summer when school was out. We took turns leading the way. There was a little river with steep banks you'd come to if you went far enough. Holmes Run, it was called. We loved it.

Sara was as fascinated with the woods as I was. There was nothing dark and sinister about them, just cool and shady and green, with terrific crackling sounds as Sara tromped through them. On pretty days the sunlight filtered through the trees and made a series of warm spotlights. Sara would put her hand in the slender shaft of sunshine and then draw it away, studying the play of light. I always stood by watching her. And if she started to go too far into the woods, I'd turn back toward home. She'd call me to come with her, but I'd just sit still, refusing to go farther.

"Too far, Sara," I'd say. "Time to head home." Sara would sigh and come back and follow me as I led the way. She was level headed and strong and vigorous, her "sturdiest child," Mama would say. But she was still a child. It was up to me to look after her.

Of course, the woods were my hunting ground, and I knew them and all that lived in them much better than Sara. I was well fed at home, but that didn't stop the yearning to patiently stalk my prey. There were baby snakes and moles and mice to hunt. Even the bugs were interesting to catch under my quick paw. It was like a game; whoever was the stealthiest won. And I usually did.

We played outside all day during the summer. Sara had a beautiful Schwinn bicycle, shimmery turquoise. Daddy got it for her one Saturday, not even for her birthday or anything. "Why should she always get Shaun's hand-me-downs?" he said. Sara would pump up the steep hill toward the bus stop and then coast down and let the wind dry her hair, up and down, again and again. Later, we'd lie in the grass, and Sara would spin stories from the clouds. Sara had a vivid imagination and could see people and animals and trees in the clouds. Sometimes I looked up, but mostly I just lay next to her and purred to show I was listening.

But the most magical of all were the summer evenings, when we could go out and play after

dinner—Sara, her sisters, and all the kids from our street. The katydids strummed us a symphony, and I felt their call right to the marrow of my bones. The night sounds were so exciting. And the fireflies would draw their silent lace until it dissolved against the night sky. The sky started out the color of her Schwinn, but it turned into the color midnight blue, Sara said.

At night the kids would play hide-and-seek. No one ever seemed to notice that I played too. When they called "all eee-all-eee-in-come-FREE-oh," everyone would assemble. They usually found the kid who hid. But they never found me, because I hid in this very pipe. So I was the winner, really.

And when it got too dark, Sara would insist that I come in. "Too many things outside at night. Time to go," she'd say. And I'd slip by her for a little while, too entranced by the katydids to follow her home. A little more time with the katydids, Sara. Just a little more, please. Exasperated, she'd pick me up tightly against her chest, hooking her left arm firmly under my shoulders and her right arm under my hips, so my paws and head faced down. I knew she was right, but sometimes I squirmed anyway. I couldn't get away, though, and that was that.

She would smell like play sweat on those nights, and when I licked her, I could taste the salt. But by bedtime she smelled like soap and fresh-washed summer pajamas.

"Beauregaaaarrrrrd! Kitty—Kitty—Kitty—KitEEE? Beau, boy! Beauregaaaarrrrrd!

KitEEE?

Doggone it, there she went again. She'd been calling all morning.

Why was she so insistent on finding me when I was having so much fun? I'd stayed out in the snow plenty of times; getting home in the fluffy little drifts was half the fun. I'll come soon, Sara. Don't worry. Soon.

Oh, the adventures and misadventures we'd had while I was growing up! I could tumble them over in my mind like a kaleidoscope.

CHAPTER 2

Doll Dresses, Respect, and Secret Rubber Bands

When I was a year old, Sara and her friend dressed me up in a doll dress. It had little pink flowers and pink trim around the collar. Sara gently threaded my arms through the little puff sleeves and buttoned it around my neck and all the way down the back. The little dress was gathered on the bodice and puffed out big all around the bottom. The neck and arms fit me perfectly.

When they put me down, they thought the effect was wonderful, but I was so mortified I wished the ground would swallow me up. There

I was—a proud, young athlete, wearing a doll dress! I hunkered down and tried to crawl under the bed. But Sara picked me up like a baby and walked outside in front of the whole universe.

The embarrassment was more than I could stand, and I jumped down and fled, searching for the first place to hide my disgrace, with the ridiculous dress billowing all around me. I ran as fast as I could, trying to make it come off, but it wouldn't.

That's when Mama saw. Goodness, what a scene.

"You get that dress off Beauregard this instant!" I'd never heard her so angry.

I let them catch me in the neighbor's yard, and Sara unbuttoned the hideous dress. I was glad to be out of that stinky old thing. But I felt sorry for her.

"You come over here right now."

"Yes, Mama." Oh boy, Sara was in big trouble.

"What were you thinking, putting a doll dress on Beauregard?"

"Well, Mama, we just thought—"

"Is he a doll?"

"Well no, Mama, but I saw it in a book, and I thought it'd be cute, and—"

"Is he a baby? Yes or no. Answer me."

"No, Mama."

"Is he even a girl?"

"No, Mama, he's not a girl."

"I want you to understand something, Sara. You humiliated Beauregard. That's a very, very bad thing."

"We didn't mean to, Mama."

"Did you even think about his feelings at all? Did *he* think it was cute to wear a dress?"

"No, Mama, I guess not. I'm sorry. I didn't think he'd mind. I would never hurt Beauregard, Mama."

"Sara, you hurt his feelings, and feelings count."

"I'm sorry, Mama."

"You were *disrespectful* to Beauregard, Sara."

"Mama, I didn't mean to be. I love Beauregard."

There was a pause while Mama thought how to explain. Then she spoke very carefully. She didn't sound mad anymore, just very, very serious.

"Sara, without respect, 'love' is just an empty word."

Mama always said that words could create and destroy, and you could never take them back.

There were no more doll dresses after that.

And that night, in bed, Sara picked me up next to her face and whispered, "I'm sorry I embarrassed you, Beauregard. I didn't mean to hurt your feelings."

"Me-eh," I whispered back with my breathy meow sound. "Me-eh. I love you. Don't worry." I stretched luxuriously on the clean-smelling sheets and sighed. All was right. And we both went to sleep in our safe red-gingham world.

"Beauregard! Kit-eeeeeeeeeee—Kit-eeeeeee-eeeee—Kit-eeeeeeeeee?"

There she was again, calling me. Oh, the long snowflakes were still so fun to watch! They were coming down thicker, but there was no need to leave. Maybe I'd wait just a little more.

Then there was the time Mama found my rubber bands. It was on a Saturday morning.

She was vacuuming the big rectangular area rug in the living room. She always cleaned under the edges. But that day she flipped the rug back farther than usual.

I kept one rubber band in the middle of each side of the rectangle, four rubber bands in all. They were the long, skinny light brown ones that weigh almost nothing. It had taken me weeks to collect them from around the house, but they were easy to hide, once I found them.

Every day I pulled back the rug with one paw and got a rubber band out with the other. Then I sat and tossed it over my head, spinning it with two paws like a pizza dough. When I'd played with one long enough, I'd pick the rug back up and put the rubber band back in its place. Then it was on to the next one, all the way around the room. Sara discovered my secret when she was

practicing the piano, but we both pretended she didn't see. The secret was part of the fun.

But when I went to play with them that day, all four of them were gone. I was heartsick.

Sara saw and came to help.

"Mama, do you know what happened to the rubber bands under the big rug?"

"You know, I found rubber bands under the rug this morning. It was the strangest thing. One on each side, right in the middle. I didn't know what to think. I threw them away."

"Mama, those are Beauregard's rubber bands. He keeps them there. He plays with each one; then he puts them back in their spots so they'll be there for next time."

Mama just shook her head in amazement. "Well, if that doesn't beat all. I'm sorry, Sara; I didn't know. See if you can find four more and put them back."

Sara managed to find three of the skinny brown ones I loved and one fat red rubber band from a newspaper. She put them back, and I played with them while we pretended she didn't see. The fat red one had ink stains and was too heavy to fly. But I pretended to play with it, just to be polite. Sara had tried hard.

After that the rubber bands were always there, even after spring cleaning.

"Beauregard. Kit-eeeee, Kit-eeeeeee, Kit-eeeeeeeeeeee?"

Gosh, it was Sara again. Oh, the snowflakes were still so glorious. They were coming down faster, but they were still so lovely and so long, like several flakes hooked together. I really shouldn't make Sara wait much longer. I'll just tell you quickly about this other time.

CHAPTER 3

Momma Birds, Neighbors, and Compromise

O nce a momma mockingbird came after me. It all started with the retired army general who lived next door. He and his wife had bird feeders, and they kept them filled with fancy seeds. In the quiet evenings, they loved to sit and watch the colorful songbirds flit back and forth, a cloud of them, enjoying the nightly feast.

The wife was always nice, but the general hated me. He called me "that cat."

I watched the birds constantly, and sometimes I even stalked them; it was just my nature. I never actually caught the silly old things.

One time I was in their yard watching a fascinating nest of baby mockingbirds. The momma worked hard to feed them, flying back and forth.

The next thing I knew, that momma bird swooped down and started pecking my head. Her beak was like a knife, and I thought she'd hammer it right through my skull. I ran into our yard and streaked across it as fast as I could, but the bird stuck with me, flying an inch above me, screaming and pecking for all she was worth. I never knew birds were so strong or so mean or that they could peck and scream so fiercely and fly at the same time.

Sara heard the commotion and came running out of the house, flapping her arms and screaming at the bird to leave me alone. The momma bird didn't give up right away. Finally she did. There were a bunch of big raw places on my head where she'd pecked my fur right off, so I was bleeding. Sara took me inside and showed Mama.

"Look what that bird did to him, Mama. His poor head!"

"She was just protecting her babies, Sara. Wash his head gently, and leave it alone. He'll heal up just fine as long as he doesn't keep getting pecked."

I made it my business not to get pecked again.

That evening the general came and knocked on the door loudly and yelled about me stalking his birds. We could hear Mama talking to him politely. When he left Sara went straight to Mama and said I was only watching, not hurting a thing.

"We have to respect our neighbors, Sara. They love their birds just like we love Beauregard. We'll put a bell on Beauregard's collar so the birds can hear him coming. That'll put the general at ease, and we can all get along."

"But, Mama, Beauregard doesn't want a bell on his collar."

"It's a compromise, Sara. We have to be considerate. Not everyone loves cats. This will keep the peace."

And it did. I got used to wearing my collar and bell, too. But I never really liked that neighbor. And although she never said a word, I don't think Mama liked him either.

MIDMORNING

"Sara, go outside, and look for Beauregard again. Call all around, back behind the house too."

"I'll go right now, Mama."

And so here she was, scrunching around in the woods with the snowy tree shapes piled thick. It was a long shot, but he might be back here; you never know. She'd already called up and down the street, again and again, even all the way back in the cul-de-sac where she'd rarely seen him.

Then she went across the street to her friend's yard, where he ran ahead of her every morning on the way to school. He waited while she rang the doorbell; then she and her friend walked together to the corner, where the three of them turned left to walk up the steep hill to the bus stop. There was nothing to the right but the big, flat area where the storm sewer was, where they congregated in the summer nights. But she called as she went by anyway.

Still there was no sign of Beauregard. It was puzzling; he was really good about coming home. OK, she would try up the hill then, past the spot where he waited for her most afternoons, her loyal friend, waiting to greet her at the bottom of the hill and then walk her home from school. She was the only kid who was met by a cat, her own welcoming committee, sixteen pounds of fun.

Beauregard was good and strong, and she'd seen him trot home in the snow before. Maybe he was in the house after all, just making mischief, or in the garage; she'd take a good look there.

He might be in the rafters, but he'd never climb these trees for sure. Too much snow.

The big, fat flakes were falling thicker and faster, faster than she'd ever seen. And the snow was still pretty but not as fluffy as it had been. It was time to get him inside.

Then there was my "colorful accident." I'll just tell you this one last story, and then I'll go.

I always slept inside, snuggled into bed with Sara. But during the day, I was free to come and go as I pleased; Mama let me in and out constantly.

I had a litter box at first, but I'd long since outgrown it. Going to the bathroom outside was immensely preferable.

One Saturday I was exploring a corner of the garage, leisurely watching a bug. The entire family was busy packing the car, getting ready for some outing. Then suddenly the big garage door closed with a bang. I'd been so distracted by the bug that I'd forgotten to show them I was there. I was locked in! But I had my water bowl, and I'd already eaten. No big deal, I thought. They'll be back soon.

But the hours went by, and no family appeared. It was nice and cool in the garage, but after a while I needed to go to the bathroom, and there was no litter box.

I waited and waited and held it and held it, straining to hear the car coming down the street. The pressure in my lower belly turned from an ache to a pain. Still I held it, clenching my bottom tightly shut.

But finally I just couldn't hold it any longer. I had to make a doo-doo. But where?

I searched through the entire garage for the most private place. It felt so uncivilized even to consider such a thing. Maybe I could hide it, and no one would find it for a long time. The back-right corner of the garage was farthest away from the lawn mower and the bikes and all the other things our family used.

I stuck my bottom as far into the corner as I could and did what I had to do. But I felt terribly ashamed. I was a big boy now, not a kitten, and holding it until you could get to a bathroom was what grown boys did.

And it smelled! It was different when I went outside; I quickly covered it with dirt and leaves and then walked away, all nice and neat with no smell. This was bad!

I scratched at the garage floor feverishly, but there it sat, a gruesome mess, the worst thing I'd ever done.

Maybe I could find a way to cover it, at least.

I searched all over and found some scraps of torn construction paper from an art project; they'd fluttered to the floor beside the trash can when Sara threw them away. The trash can was on the same wall as my horrible doo-doo, but at the opposite end, near the front of the garage.

I worked diligently to move the scraps from one end of the garage to the other, dragging each piece with my paw, little by little, across the slick cement floor. It was slow work because I couldn't pick them up. I brought a red scrap first, then a green, and then a yellow. I arranged them carefully over the offending pile, as close together as I could.

There, you couldn't even see it. That was much better. I felt relieved. Maybe no one would even notice.

I snoozed and waited.

Finally the garage door went up, and everyone piled out of the car, chattering and unloading things.

Mama had only taken a step before she stopped and sniffed the air.

"What's that smell? Something stinks. It smells like dog doo. Where's that coming from?"

I knew then it was no use to hide. My ruse had failed. I walked out and sat in front of Mama.

"Sara, was Beauregard locked in here all day? Did he *go* in here?"

Sara followed her nose to the pile.

Gosh, Mama was fit to be tied! Going to the bathroom in the house was forbidden.

I looked at my crazy patchwork cover-up and hung my head. It had seemed like such a good idea at the time, but now it just looked stupid. My face burned red under my black coat.

Sara stepped in front of me, standing between her angry parent and me.

"But, Mama, he was stuck in here all day. And look how hard he tried to cover it up! Those paper scraps, they must have been by the trash can. He moved them all the way here, one by one. It must have taken him a long time."

Mama wasn't having it, not one bit. It was time for desperate measures. Sara took a deep breath and tried again.

"Why, it's so colorful! You know, if you look at it the right way, it's almost like—a pinwheel."

That one stopped Mama. Daddy was a lawyer, but none of us had ever heard of the "pinwheel defense." I could see her trying to keep a stern face.

"Well, it sure doesn't smell like a pinwheel!"

"I want you to clean it up immediately, Sara, so clean you'd never know it was there. And from now on, you'll have to make sure he doesn't get locked in the garage. Never again, OK?"

"Yes, Mama."

And so my nasty doo-doo was disposed of.

The next morning I needed to go to the bathroom early, before it was quite light. I tried to wake Sara, but she was sleeping too soundly. Besides, she was still growing and needed her rest.

I padded down the hall to Mama and stood on my hind legs, reaching my soft paw up to her face. I patted her cheek as softly as I could. Pat, pat, pat, Mama. Wake up, please.

And she did and silently walked down the stairs and let me out the front door so I could go.

It was Sara's job to let me out, but Mama did it every day from then on. Her bark was worse than her bite. It was our little secret.

Sara Looks High and Low

MIDDAY

It was hard to win a game of hide-and-seek with Beauregard. He seemed to be able to invent spaces you never knew existed and then insinuate his big, strong body into them. He'd step into the room from who knew where, like a black, satin Houdini. And when they played outside, he would materialize out of the air itself, a barely perceptible black shape sitting silently against the backdrop of midnight blue twilight.

She decided to search the laundry room again, behind the water heater where she'd found him once, and then in the back of the washer and dryer, peering carefully with a flashlight. There was nothing behind the laundry basket or in the far corner that never got used.

Where could he be?

CHAPTER 5

My Hideous Mistake

Well, there was no getting around it. The wind was picking up; I could hear it. It was time to put daydreams aside and get moving. I'd have to trot through the wet snow to go home. Fluffy snow was fine, the powdery kind you could shake off easily. But this stuff had turned cold and icky, and it had piled up several inches, too, higher than I'd meant to let it get. I'd daydreamed too long. No problem; I'll just paw through it and make a run for it. I'll be back in the warm kitchen soon enough. Mama will be waiting to let me in.

But somehow since I last looked out, something had gone terribly wrong. The pretty snowdrift was higher than I thought it would be, and it had moved. I couldn't even poke my head out, just my nose. Then I'll move the snow; I've done it before. I can even tunnel through, if I have to.

But when I pawed the drift, it didn't respond. It had turned into a heavy white wall I couldn't get through. The long flakes had cemented themselves, locked together with wet and cold.

I scraped at the wall furiously, digging with my strong claws for all I was worth. How could this have happened to me? This was impossible! Maybe it was just a nightmare, not real at all. But it was real. I felt a hideous fear rising in me for the first time in my life. It tasted so bitter; it burned my throat.

Wait, wait, wait! There was an opening at the other end of the pipe. Try there, silly! It was a little longer way home but still doable. Go, go, go!

As I raced to the other end of the cold pipe, I noticed how black it was. Where was the sunlight? There should be some. Then I slammed at full speed into the other opening, sealed shut with more freezing snow. It didn't hurt; I was too frantic for it to hurt.

OK then, turn around. Try again! I raced back to the other end. There was still a little gray light, several inches at the top; I could see it. Start over. I'd climb out somehow, even if I had to squish down flat like a hamster. I climbed feverishly. I bit at it. But I couldn't get out.

No, no, no, no, no! How could I be trapped here, in my favorite spot?

I backed up and raced ahead, slamming my shoulder into the bank of snow like a battering ram. Again and again and again, I rammed it. I'm Beauregard, Beauregard! This can't be happening, not to me. I want to go home. It's time to go home. My home's just down the street!

But nothing changed. The icy white wall refused to yield to any of my tricks or all the weight I hurled at it. It was as impenetrable as the slick garage floor. I sat back and put my head up and howled a deep scream of rage and frustration. I'd never screamed before. I knew I sounded like an animal, but I was too full of black terror to care. My scream surrounded me and banged around inside the pipe, echoing back again and again.

Outside, the wind returned my howl, easily screaming louder than I ever could. And the wind didn't sound scared at all. It just swept more and more snow against the fast-closing pipe.

And I knew then that the pipe was my tomb.

I was being buried alive.

CHAPTER 6

My Terror and
Mama's Teachings

The freezing, black pipe crouched behind me like a predator, baiting me with my own despair, hungering for me to give up. But I wasn't ready yet. My paws were beginning to hurt from the cold. They weren't numb at all, not even a little. They hurt so much.

You know, people tell all kinds of stories about cats, like the one about having nine lives, as if each were inconsequential or somehow disposable. But I assure you, I'm as dearly attached to my one life on this earth as you are to yours.

I wanted so desperately to live, if only I could figure out how! What would Mama say to do? I searched my mind. Mama always knew what to do. Yes, I remembered. She said, "Your mind is always your best weapon. If you ever get into real trouble, remember to stay calm and use your head." I'd heard her say it to Sara and her sisters.

Think! Think hard! What do you have left to work with? Don't waste time feeling sorry for yourself. Think it through, and use whatever power you have left.

Whatever power I have left, I pondered. I didn't have enough physical strength to claw my way out of the pipe. But I still had a voice. And I wasn't too far from home.

I cleared my head and promised myself I wouldn't go down without a fight. I would fight with all I had left. And all I had left was my voice.

"Help me; I'm trapped!" I yelled, straining to put my lips up to the opening, only about five inches left.

Stop. Breathe. Try again. Yell at even intervals.

"HELLLLLLLLPPPPPPPPPP!"

Inhale the icy air. Rest a second.

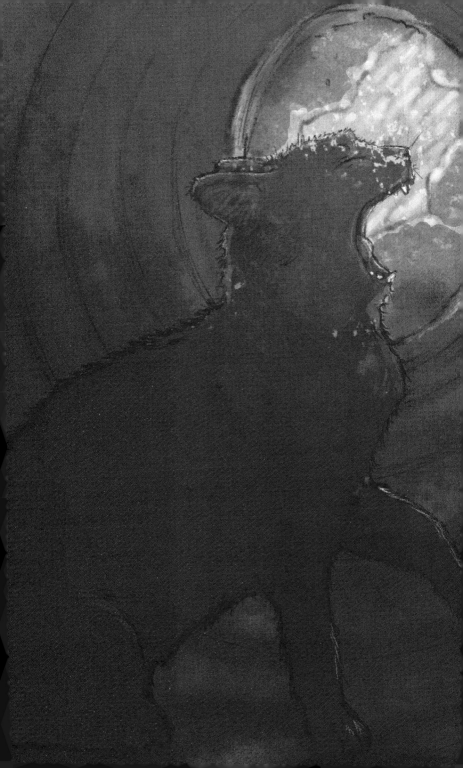

Again.

"Anybody, HELLLLPPPPPPPP!"

And I continued with my desperate regimen. I don't know how long it was. I yelled a thousand times and more. My throat was raw, and my paws were starting to hurt terribly.

The storm churned furiously outside. I had never heard such wind; it seemed deafening, even in here. The hours of Sara searching for me were over. But maybe some grown-up was outside, close enough to hear.

"HELLLLLLP! I'm trapped in the pipe. HELLLLLLLLLPPPPPPP!"

I felt as helpless as a worm that thrashes to get off the hot sidewalk, doomed to die simply because it had stayed too long in a place it shouldn't have been.

"HELLLLLLP! I'm trapped in the pipe. HELLLLLLLLLPPPPPPP!"

Oh, please, dear Creator, not like this. Please don't let my sweet my life end like this.

CHAPTER 7

Sara's Search Becomes Urgent

EARLY AFTERNOON

She'd start again at the top of the house, the far-right corner, and work across the upstairs, and then down.

"Keep looking," Mama had said.

He went out early this morning to do his business, like always. She was pretty sure he'd come back in; Beauregard came and went so freely it was hard to keep track.

She looked once more upstairs under the red-gingham bed, under her dresser and school desk, in the closet behind the toys, every inch of her room.

Then it was on to the other rooms once more: behind the piano in the living room; underneath all the beds, Shaun's and Caroline's, and Mama and Daddy's; behind the other dressers; behind the toilets; behind the shower curtains; behind the books in the bookshelves. He could fit full grown into any crevice that could hold a kitten; it was part of his magic.

If she didn't find him soon, she'd have to try outside again, wet snowsuit and all. The snow was falling thicker and faster, and Mama said it was time to get him in. She kept looking out the kitchen window for him. Come on now, Beauregard. This isn't funny anymore.

CHAPTER 8

Mama's Dilemma

It was the kind of weather that made people call off search-and-rescue efforts, not begin them. Now here was her level-headed middle daughter wanting to leave the house.

"Mama, I'm going out to look for Beauregard. He's not inside. I've looked everywhere, again and again. Under the beds, behind the piano, everywhere. In the garage, too, just like you said. He's not here."

Mama had been standing at the window of the kitchen door for the last two hours watching the furious storm gain momentum, hoping against hope that her beloved cat-boy would somehow make his way home. She'd sent Sara back to search the house repeatedly, buying time.

She'd decided to keep Sara inside hours ago. Now even the radio said to stay inside. She dreaded telling her the truth. Beauregard would have to make it on his own, or not. It was too late to go out in the storm.

As she turned away from the turbulent scene outside, she was shocked that even Sara would think of leaving the snug house. She knew she was devoted to Beauregard, but the very idea of leaving the house was insane. The storm was phenomenal; it was slamming ice pellets against the window and shaking the door right now. The storm could eat her alive. No one would go out there. No one.

Shaun and Caroline were sitting at the kitchen table, bewildered that Sara would ask such a thing.

Kind but firm, she told herself. Deep breath.

"Sara, I'm sorry; you can't go outside. This is a bad storm, a very, very serious storm. I can't allow you to go out in it. It's just too dangerous."

Now it was Sara's turn to be shocked. It had never occurred to her she'd be denied the chance to try outside again.

"But, Mama, something's wrong. I know it. I just know it! He would have come home by now. I've got to go out and look for him. I've got to!"

You're the mother. Keep trying. Be firm. Be patient. She doesn't understand.

"He's probably holed up in someone's garage, Sara. Beauregard's a smart cat. You'll see. He'll come trotting home as soon as he can make it through the snow. Maybe tomorrow. Or maybe even a week from now. Sometimes cats will show up weeks after they've disappeared. We haven't given up on him, not by a long shot, but you have to stay inside."

"Please, Mama, please! Something's wrong. I have to find him, please!"

Mama's heart sank. Sara had never begged her before. They had a nice home, and they respected each other. No one ever begged. There had never been a reason to beg.

"Please, Mama, just one more time. Please, Mama, please! Just one more time. Please, Mama. Please let me look for him one more time. Please let me go. Mama, Please!

"Sara, I'm sorry. It's just too dangerous."

Now, make it final.

"I forbid it."

Sara turned to leave the kitchen, defeated, the very picture of misery. She'd go upstairs and cry, but it wouldn't bring her friend back.

But before she'd taken the second step, something came over her, and she turned on Mama, closing the distance of authority between parent and child.

Sara herself was still the same girl, but she was fearless. Leaving Beauregard alone outside was wrong; she knew it. She lived to find him. Nothing else mattered. It made her Mama's equal.

"But, Mama, he'll DIE out there!"

The words came hurling out of her all by themselves and then filled every inch of the warm kitchen.

Sara's conviction was unassailable, so strong it seemed to take on a life of its own. It was a force of nature in itself.

Confusion flickered across Mama's pretty features. Then her face hung in despair, as if she might burst into tears.

She looked out again at the furious storm. Sara's conviction had swayed her.

Sara was strong, as strong as a boy. And she'd probably turn back after she got a few feet from the house, still in the driveway, still in sight.

Best let her go outside and see for herself how futile it was. At least this way, she'd know she'd tried her hardest to save him. If they never saw

Beauregard again, it would be her only comfort. If she felt like she'd betrayed him, she'd never get over it.

She turned back to her daughter, grim and determined.

"I'll let you look for him one more time."

CHAPTER 9

Fighting for My Life

"I'm trapped in the pipe!"

"Anybody, help!"

Stop. Breathe. Try again.

"Help!"

Inhale the icy air. Rest a second.

Again.

"I'm snowed in. I'm in the pipe."

"Anybody, help."

"Help me, please!"

Stop. Inhale. Try again.

You have nothing to lose.

It's your only chance.

"I'm snowed in. I'm in the pipe."

"Anybody, help."

"Help me, PLEEEEEEEEASE, please!"

CHAPTER 10

Beauregard's Family Takes Action

The world righted itself. Mama was in charge again.

"Shaun and Caroline, run get her snowsuit and her boots. Make sure they're good and dry. Use a towel and dry them out."

"Bring dry scarves, hats and mittens, and warm dry socks. All you can. I'll pick the best ones."

"Quick, hurry," she ordered. "Run! There isn't much time. Run!"

And as they raced to obey, Mama and Sara stood side by side and watched the storm grow more powerful, piling the relentless snow higher by the minute.

Sara stood like a scarecrow as her mother and sisters worked to wrap her in warm clothes as fast as they could.

Mama barked the directions: a wool sweater, corduroy pants, wool hat pulled down over her ears, and then a wool scarf wrapped around her neck.

"Faster. Move faster. There's no time left."

"Heavy wool socks on her feet. Quick, get her snow boots dry inside. Good."

"Now help her get the snow pants on. Now the boots. Stuff her pants all the way down in the boots. All the way down."

"Hurry."

"Now her snowsuit jacket. Bring the hood up good and loose. Pull it out over the wool hat so it stays in place over her ears. Now pull the drawstring tight down around her face, as tight as you can. Tie it in a double knot. It can't come undone."

"Put her mittens on. Now pull her sleeves out and down over them, carefully, down to her wrists. Let go. There."

And when all the normal measures were taken, Mama turned Sara around and stood behind her. "Stand perfectly still."

She tied another wool scarf firmly over her nose and chin, a measure never taken before.

"You can breathe through the scarf; all you have to do is see," Mama said.

The red snowsuit cocoon was complete.

She turned Sara around, took her by the shoulders, and looked down into her face.

"You can't just stay out there. If you can't find him pretty soon, you have to come home. And you have to stay in the road; you can't go back in the woods."

"Promise me."

Sara nodded her agreement, and Mama opened the door for her. A firestorm of ice and snow reached in and broke the warmth of the kitchen.

And as her frightened sisters watched in amazement, Sara stepped out into it.

CHAPTER 11

The Storm

An explosion of icy air hit her first, blasting straight up from the ground. It stole her breath and her stomach, a thrill like you feel on a roller coaster, but not the fun kind.

She recovered from the shock and started up the driveway. The snowdrifts were up to her knees, but Sara could handle the snow; she'd walked in deep snow many times. But the wind was a different story altogether. It roared like a locomotive and surged like one, too, tearing in circles around her, first one way and then the other, reversing on itself, clutching at her legs, beating around her head. It felt bewildering. Every time she adjusted for it, it came out of a new direction. But she concentrated hard and was able to push forward.

Now that she was out, she didn't really know where to look. There was nothing behind the house except woods, and she'd promised to stay in the road. So she decided to head up the sloping driveway to the street. It was hard going, but she could do it.

Turning left out of the driveway would take her back toward the cul-de-sac. But Beauregard seldom went that way, only as far as her friend's house a few doors down.

So she decided to turn right out of the driveway, toward the big hill that turned left at the end of the street and led up to the bus stop. Beau liked the hill.

She'd never felt anything like the raging wind. It turned the icy snow into driving pellets that stung her eyes too hard to look ahead. She struggled forward with her head down, stopping every few steps to look up and check her course, then putting her head down and starting again.

She could see enough to know where she was, but the wind was deafening. And it kept getting louder, which seemed impossible.

"BEAUREGAAAAAARRRRRRRRR-RRRD! KITEEEEEEEEEE, KITTEEEEE-EEEEEEE, KITTEEEEEEEEEE? BEAURE-GAARRRRRRD!"

She called as loudly as she could, but the wind overpowered her voice effortlessly. Her cries evaporated the moment they left her.

CHAPTER 12

Sara's Screams Reach Me

And that was when I heard it, a faint cry, interrupted, coming in and out like a voice on Shaun's transistor radio, the terrible wind stealing the rest. But I'd know that voice anywhere.

"Beau—garrrrrrrrrd—eeeeeeeee! Kit—gaa-aaarrrddd…"

It was Sara! Oh, dear Creator, how had she managed to come out in the storm? How could Mama have let her come out in this?

Relief washed over me like a warm balm, and I felt it fueling me from head to toe.

"Sara, I'm here." I was jubilant. "I'm here in the pipe."

"Kit—y. Beau—gard. B—regard."

"Kitty. KiteeeEEEEEEEEE!

She was getting closer, but the calls only continued. Sara couldn't hear me over the deafening wind.

I put my lips up to the pipe as closely as I could. There were only a few inches left before the freezing snow would shut out the last inches of dim, gray light.

I slowly filled my lungs like a bellows, inhaling every last drop of the icy, black air. Carefully, right down to the bottom of your lungs, put every single air sac to use. Make it count.

"Sara, I'm here in the pipe!"

Inhale again. Down deep. Sara, please hear me. Oh, please, Sara.

"Sara, can't you hear me?"

Wait for a pause in the wind. Wait for the roar to subside a little. Now!

"Sara, I'm here in the pipe!"

"Kit—yeeeee! Beau—gaaaaarrrddd. B—re-gaaaarrrrd! Kiteeeeeeeeeeee! KiteeeEEEEEE-EEE!"

CHAPTER 13

No Turning Back

What a strange world it was out here. The storm seemed to hate her—a personal hate, wicked and vengeful. This didn't seem to be about any kind of weather. The elements seemed bent on showing her how much they despised her. It was a shock to feel despised.

"Kiteeeeeeeeee, Kitteeeeeeeeeee, Kitteeeeeeeeee! Beau......Beauregaarrrrrrd!" Kiteeeeeeeeee?"

She'd made it almost to the end of the street, breathing hard. Her legs were starting to get a little tired, but she still felt strong, and she wasn't cold. There was no one in sight and certainly no Beauregard. The only sound was the hurtling wind, impossibly loud and then louder still.

Keep going. Keep looking. But where?

Well, she wasn't going back yet; that was for sure. OK, so head for the corner, look up and see it. OK, there it is. Now go.

"Kiteeee_____   eeeee____eeee!   Kit_____ eeeee,   Kitteeeeeeeeee!   Beau,   Beaureg_____ rrrd! _____teeee_____eeee?"

Sara, I'm here in the big pipe. The storm sewer."

"I'm snowed in."

"Sara, I'm here. Right here!"

"Please, Sara, I'm here in the pipe. Sara, please hear me!"

Now she was at the corner. Call again.

"Beau—Beauregard. Kitty? Beauregaaaaaarr-rrrrrd!"

She heard nothing. She stopped calling and listened as hard as she could. There was only the roaring of the vast white inferno. How could anything be alive in this?

Maybe Mama was right; this was useless.

No, it was still too soon to give up. Too soon. Keep trying.

Breathe. Catch your breath. Start up the hill. Keep calling. Take a deep breath. Make it as loud as you can.

"Beauregard. Kitty, Kitty, Kittteeeeeeeee?"

"Beau—Beauregard. Kitty? Beauregard. Kitty, Kitty, Kitttteeeeeee?"

"Beaurregarrrd!"

She was passing right by me. She was at the corner, right across the street. Oh, how can she be so close and not hear me?

Again, slowly, fill deep, deep down. Every last air sac. Now try.

"Sara, I'm here in the sewer pipe. Right here, Sara, pleeeeeeease! I'm on your right, Sara! Here in the pipe! Right here!"

She was halfway up the hill when she heard it, a tiny squeak amid the furious bellowing of the wind.

It couldn't be Beauregard; Beauregard didn't squeak.

Was she imagining it?

Listen hard. Listen as hard as you can. She strained to hear. There it was again, just barely audible but there.

The wind tore around her head in circles. Was it her left ear she could hear the squeak in? Yes, it was to her left, up the hill.

It didn't sound a thing like Beauregard, but it was the only sound other than the deafening wind.

Turn left up the hill.

"Beaureg—rd? Kit—e—e? Ki____eeeeeee?"

No, no, no. No! She'd turned the wrong way up the hill.

"Sara, I'm here. I'm in the pipe. Down the hill, Sara."

"You're going the wrong way! I'm right here! Saraaaaaaaa!"

Stop. Wait for a break in the wind. Wait.
Now try!
"Sara, I'm here. I'm in the pipe!.
"Down the hill, Sara!
"Sara, down --- down the hill!"

She stood and strained to hear the infinitesimal squeak. If the wind would only hush for a second, maybe she could figure it out.

"Sara, please! I'm here in the storm pipe. I'm stuck. Sara. Sara you're going the wrong way!"

There! There it was. But it was from her right ear that she heard it this time. Listen. Yes, it was coming from her right, not her left. It was coming from the corner she'd just passed, the big, flat place where they played at night.

But Beauregard didn't make a sound like that; it couldn't be him.

Stop. Breathe. Now fill your lungs again. Inhale slowly, all the way to the bottom.

"Sara, you passed me! I'm here in the storm pipe. Down here in the pipe, Sara! Sara!"

It wasn't even really a squeak, just the hint of one. She could still barely make it out.

It couldn't be Beauregard.

But because it was the only sound in the white universe other than the outraged wind, Sara turned back down the hill and made her way toward it. She didn't know what else to do.

CHAPTER 14

A Game of Marco Polo

Her cries stopped. She was coming closer. She must have turned back down the hill. She heard me!

"Beauree—aarrrrr—d!"

Try again. Go slowly. Feel the ice to the bottom of your lungs.

Now scream for all you're worth.

"Saraaaaaaaa, I'm in the pipe! The pipe, Sara!"

"Beauregarrrrrrrrrrrrrrrrrd!"

She sounded a little closer.

"Sara! I'm here, in the pipe!"

"Beauregarrrrrdddddd!"

She was closer still.

"Saraaaaaaaaa! I'm in the pipe!"

"Beauregarrrrrrddddd! Beaureg_____rrrd? Kittt_____eee____eeee? Kit____eeeeeeee?"

And on we went, playing a desperate game of Marco Polo in the blinding storm. The wind was so loud I couldn't tell how close she was.

"Oh please, Saraaaaaa, I'm in the pipe!"

And then she was there, the most beautiful girl in the world. She peered down into the pipe as I yelled my head off. Her face was completely covered with an icy scarf. All I could see were her eyes, with snow frozen on her eyelashes.

I opened my eyes wide so she could see me in the blackness.

It was enough.

Somehow in the midst of the murderous storm, Sara had found me. She was here, as strong and capable as ever. And now she'd take me home. I wanted to tell her how much I loved her and that no one ever had a better friend in the whole universe.

But all I could say was "Get me outta here!"

My Best Friend
Rescues Me

Sara went to work immediately, trying to shovel the snowdrift back with her mittens. She couldn't move it with one hand like normal snow. It was as heavy as wet cement.

She quickly started a new method: left hand down on the drift, right hand on top, push down, pull back hard with two hands, left hand down, push with right, pull back with two. Again and again and again and again and again.

Finally she made an opening big enough to reach in and pull me out. Oh, thank you, dear Creator, thank you!

She anchored me high against her chest with her arms. Her left arm hooked under my shoulders, her right arm under my hips. It was our normal way.

I noticed she was already breathing hard. But that was fine; Sara didn't mind breathing hard.

All she said was "Let's go."

CHAPTER 16

Out of the Pipe and into Hell

When she stood up, I realized instantly that Sara had come out into hell to find me, and now we were in hell together. The magnitude of the storm was shocking. The ice and snow were an onslaught, but the worst tormentor was the wind. It lashed us from every direction, enthralled with its own power. It felt like it would sear my coat right off me. I couldn't tell if it would freeze me or burn me alive. The sheer force of it was far more sinister than the snowdrifts, which shifted around us like glittering quicksand.

The morning's snowflake pillows had turned into ice pellets that shot at us like BBs. I squeezed my eyes shut and hung gratefully in Sara's arms. How could she even see?

She set out for home, moving as fast as she could, pulling her knees up high out of the snow and punching down through it. She seemed to move with her head down, sheltering me, stopping every three or four steps to look up and make sure we were heading in the right direction. The storm was getting worse by the second.

Sara was always tired when she carried me home against her chest. Sixteen pounds was a lot for her. Her arms had never been particularly strong.

But her legs were. Even with the wind tearing at us, we were making good progress, plowing through the heavy drifts. Sara could manage the snow. We'd be home in no time.

Just when I thought we were almost home free, we had another shock. A giant hand came for us, a hand made out of wind so strong it made the other gusts seem like little puffs of breath.

The hand shoved Sara roughly—deliberately—in the chest, and she started falling backward into

the turbulent snowdrifts. She struggled desperately to regain her balance.

She managed to get her feet back under her without an instant to spare, and I felt her push forward into the wind with every muscle in her body, all her normal muscles and then muscles neither of us ever knew she had.

Summoned into service, she seemed to have muscles even in her teeth; one muscle fiber pulled into the fight after the one in front of it, painfully dredged up from deep in her body.

"You, you, you," her body seemed to say, pointing at each individual reserve. "Go now!" And the unwilling recruits responded, wrenching themselves from their lifelong slumber, called to do the work they were created for. Each brought its individual power, each with a protest of pain.

The muscle strength intended for emergency use only flowed up the back of her calves, bracing her legs against the mighty wind, willing to do its job when called, if only this once in Sara's life.

I had a sense that someone was there with us, holding her ankles in place.

Every last synapse and cell and sinew formed a trembling, unified front, but still Sara struggled to stand.

It felt like a deadly game of arm wrestling.

The wind was the palm of the giant, and Sara's chest was the opposing hand. She stood, and she stood, and she stood, pushing forward, shuddering from head to toe with the effort, every element of her being called into the fight.

The surly wind seemed intent on laughing at us, effortlessly pouring itself over and around us, daring us to stand up to it. Sara fought to stay on her feet like a drowning person struggles to keep her face above water. We had to stay upright or we wouldn't have a chance.

The drifts were too deep for Sara to crawl home in. If we fell, they'd be only too happy to swallow us.

It was not enough. More.

Push back.

More.

More pain. More strength.

More still.

I felt for the first time that my sturdy tomboy friend was just a fragile little girl. And I was even less, only an inconsequential black dot in a sea of surging white.

Despite the killing wind and her many layers of clothing, I could smell Sara's fear.

We were paralyzed, and there was no one to help us. It felt like all the anger in the world had been unleashed on the two of us. The storm was colossal, unlike anything we'd never known.

We were no match for this.

CHAPTER 17

Together

With a flourish of contempt, the giant's hand dismissed us, and Sara almost fell forward; she'd been pushing so hard. But instead of relief, my apprehension only grew. The wind hand had left so quickly it was as if it'd only been toying with us, the way I'd gleefully played with a tiny mouse, knowing full well how easily I could kill it when I was ready.

It was as if the wind had left behind an ominous threat. "Fine, you can stand for now, but when I come back, I'll show you what I'm really made of. You're nothing next to me. You didn't heed my warning; now you'll die for your audacity."

Sara stood trembling, but this time her trembling felt empty, as devoid of power as the snakeskin we'd found in the woods long ago. Our world had caressed us then; now it was bent on destroying us and laughing at us, too.

The snow seemed to crash around us, a white abyss, utterly lethal. If we fell into it, we wouldn't come out.

Sara carefully started forward again, a cautious new way this time. She had to be able to stay upright when the wind hand came back and shoved us again.

Instead of raising her knees high and plowing forward as fast as she could, she lifted one foot up slowly, keeping the standing foot as deep and solid in the snow as she could.

Then she pushed the lifted foot down until it felt solid. But there were already six inches of frozen snow on the ground before the storm hit; nothing felt even.

Our steps were less than half as long and far slower and more careful.

Take one carefully measured step. Then both feet down, ready for the wind. Get a good solid purchase.

Now take the risk—lift the back foot. Keep the front one still; it's all you've got to hold you. Be ready.

Move one foot after the other, slowly and deliberately. Get a solid footing with two; then lift again. It was a snail's pace, but we now understood how precarious any and every movement was.

Sara was quivering from head to toe, completely spent with the effort, her slender body wracked with pain.

Somehow on this day, all because I wouldn't answer Sara's early calls, we'd become the lowliest of prey. I knew now how helpless the baby mockingbirds had felt when I stalked them.

The fateful wind battered us relentlessly, and the snow shifted and swirled in ugly little cyclones around Sara's knees as I looked down. The piercing ice pellets stung our faces, one blast after another.

I was freezing, so icy cold I didn't know if I could even move.

Lift one foot. Keep your balance. Push down. Find something solid. Now again.

The vast white wasteland seemed to obliterate every effort; Sara's footprints were swept away instantly. There were countless snail steps left to take before Sara could collapse. She was terrified that the giant wind would come back, and so was I. I wanted to try moving my arms and legs—they hurt so badly. But all I could do to help Sara was hang perfectly still.

The tedious steps continued, exhausting and excruciating. First Sara's arms shook the hardest and then her legs and feet.

Sara struggled to draw a clean breath but failed again and again. She had been raised to do her very best, but that simple standard, and all other reason, had vanished with the wind hand.

I didn't know what to call this new dimension we had entered. There was nothing in it but pain and steely determination.

And the two of us.

But alone in the deadly storm, I could read Sara's mind as clearly as ever.

"I'm not sure we'll make it home, but I'm glad we're together."

CHAPTER 18

Half Steps and Agony

The turbulent white world churned around us, and Sara's tortured half steps continued. It seemed like an eternity.

The only control Sara had left was to pick up one foot. But when she planted it, her leg shook so hard that I felt only the molten snow was holding it in place.

She carefully stopped and looked up every few steps, and I was pretty sure she was on course. The ice pellets burned so badly that I couldn't stand to open my eyes.

But I could feel her arms sagging slowly toward the snow; the little cyclones bit at my feet as she bent under my weight. They must not be completely frozen, or it wouldn't hurt so much.

Suddenly she stopped and leaned over sharply, and I thought she was finally giving up. If she dropped me, I'd already forgiven her. I knew she'd tried much harder than either of us ever thought she could. At least I'd escaped the lonely, black pipe, and I was with Sara.

But she had only bent double to rest her elbows on her knees. The comforting "lub dub" in her chest that lulled me to sleep at night had long since turned to a furious hammering. Her heart banged like a piston, straining against the walls of her small rib cage. The space wasn't big enough for her heart to do its job. It pounded so hard on my back that I thought it'd break out altogether.

She heaved in and out, clawing the icy air for a clean breath, again and again and again. But the panting never improved, and the restoring breath never came.

Then she stood up quickly and pulled me up higher against her chest, as high as when we started.

She turned left decisively, ninety degrees, a real turn. The suspense was too much for me.

I opened my eyes a tiny bit and realized we were at the top of our driveway.

Sara trudged forward again, shaking like a leaf from head to toe, the deafening storm swirling its stupendous waves of wind and snow around us.

Finally I could see the light of the kitchen window.

Then I could hear Mama's voice, exultant in a way I'd never heard before. "She's got him! Oh, she's got him, girls. Look. Oh, she's got him!"

All three faces were at the window: Mama, Shaun, and Caroline. With all the blowing snow, they couldn't see Sara's trembling, and they didn't understand the fix she was in. At least if we fell now, they could come get us. But there were still many steps left to go.

Finally my feet hurt so badly that I couldn't wait any longer. I started to struggle. Let me go, Sara. Let me go! I can see them. They're about to open the door. Loosen your grip, Sara. I can jump from here. One good jump and the pain will stop. Let me go!

But Sara's arms stayed locked tight. Her job wasn't done yet.

CHAPTER 19

Homecoming

When they opened the door, Sara dove onto the floor of the warm kitchen, spilling me out of her arms.

I jumped up and down, shaking my arms and legs frantically to get the hateful snow off me.

It was a ridiculous-looking dance, I knew. But I didn't care; I was thrilled to see everything in my body worked.

Mama and Shaun and Caroline jumped up and down and clapped and cheered and laughed.

They laughed at my funny dance, and they cheered some more.

Sara lay on the floor facedown, arms and legs sprawled, her chest heaving, gasping for a real breath.

There was all the air and warmth she needed, but she couldn't draw it in.

"How'd you find him?"

"Where was he?"

"Was it hard to carry him?"

There was silence then; they were puzzled. Sara wasn't celebrating, only heaving, still struggling for a breath.

"We could see you coming."

"Is it freezing out there?"

"We couldn't believe our eyes!"

"Did you stay warm?"

There was still no answer from Sara. Finally Mama began to understand.

"Well, are you just exhausted?"

Minutes and minutes went by before Sara could speak at all.

Finally she found a ragged breath and gasped out, "He was in the storm pipe. All I could see was his eyes."

And those words became the entire story of my rescue, all anyone in our family ever said about that day, the sum total of our travail. They didn't understand what we'd been through, and they never would or could.

With all the vocabulary words Sara and I knew between us, we never even tried to explain, not about my gritty showdown with terror or my freezing pain or Sara's trembling agony.

We knew we could never communicate the horror of our journey or how close we came to dying.

And I'm still not sure I have.

The only images that would remain were my yellow eyes staring out of a black pipe and that of a young girl in a red snowsuit emerging from a violent snowstorm with my beloved black form in her arms.

And we never dwelled on how narrow my escape had been either—only inches left before my grisly fate would have been sealed.

We'd made it back because we refused to give up, first individually and then together, no matter how hard it got, just like Mama had taught us.

So if my glowing yellow eyes in the black pipe became the entire story of our ordeal, that was just fine with us.

We were home!

CHAPTER 20

A Warm Bed with Nightmares

Mama and Shaun dried me off with a big bath towel and rubbed me hard to get my circulation going. It felt wonderful to have them work on me in the warm house. Then I went and basked in front of the fireplace in the den, soaking up the heat. Mama always kept a supply of dry wood, and the hearth was always toasty. I wiggled my toes until they felt as warm as the rest of me. I'd catch up with Sara later; she knew exactly where I'd be.

They helped Sara stand up and peeled off her frozen clothes and then put her in the bathtub upstairs. "Start with a barely warm bath," Mama said. "Then add hot water a little at a time so it won't hurt." After she was good and warm, they dried her off, and she put on a flannel gown and robe and slippers.

We ate a nice dinner, just like always. Mama gave me a whole can of tuna juice to celebrate our homecoming. It was delicious, but I was almost too tired to appreciate it.

But when we went to bed, things were different.

One of my normal jobs was to comfort Sara when she woke up from a bad dream. She'd wake with a start, and I'd walk softly up from the foot of the bed and purr by her face. "Just a bad dream, Sara. Meh-eh. It's OK; go back to sleep."

But tonight the tables had turned. I couldn't relax. Sara took extra time petting me before we went to sleep, but I was still nervous and jumpy. I knew in my mind we'd made it home. Or had we? Maybe I was still in the pipe, and I was only dreaming that we were home in our bed, dreaming as I froze in the hideous blackness. Maybe my nightmare encounter with death was still real, and the cold, black predator at my back was still there, waiting for me to give up, waiting to be triumphant, silent and ever patient.

Maybe our clean, snuggly bed wasn't real. My assurance that life was safe had been shaken to the core.

Every time I drifted off to sleep, the cold, black terror came back, and I jerked into consciousness.

Sara would wake up immediately and sit up cross-legged in the bed. She petted and petted me, her consoling hands stroking me from cheekbone to hip, again and again.

Sara was back to being strong, just like she'd always been.

"It's all right, Beau. We made it home safe and sound. We're here in our bed where we belong. Everything's fine. We're not in the storm anymore. We made it."

She sang softly and she stroked and she rubbed, and by the end of the long night, I finally managed to sleep a little.

CHAPTER 21

A Dazzling Display

In the morning we woke to see a dazzling silver glacier outside. It had flowed right out of the sky and frozen solid overnight. There were no streets or curbs or driveways in sight, only the idea of our neighborhood, encased in undulating ice.

I looked out the bedroom window and felt the grip of terror instantly. My pipe tomb was sealed and buried several feet deep, and it would stay frozen shut for weeks.

What a lonely death it would have been if Sara hadn't found me. I couldn't stand to look.

But Sara was fully recovered and thrilled. She said it was like an ice palace outside. She saw thousands of tiny prisms on the ice-locked windowsill.

She picked me up on her shoulder, as cheerful and enthusiastic as ever.

"Don't worry, Beau. We're inside. Let's go downstairs and find Mama. I'm hungry."

And sheltered from the glittering ice world, our day began. I decided to stay away from the windows. No one even tried to open a door.

Mama was fixing a big breakfast; it smelled delicious: bacon and eggs and hot buttered biscuits with strawberry jam. Everyone ate until they were full, and I chowed down, too. Mama gave me a little tuna oil; we were still celebrating.

Mama made a big pot of vegetable soup for lunch and put it on the stove to simmer. She seemed happy but nervous—like me. And she kept going to the kitchen window and looking out. She went back again and again. Then she'd shake her head a little and look scared. Then she went on taking care of us.

She said it'd been a close call but that she guessed cats really did have nine lives and that's how I'd escaped. But I knew she didn't believe it. She just didn't know what else to say. The aftermath of the storm made it clear what a serious risk she'd taken by letting Sara go after me. It was a hard decision, but our family was intact because of it.

Mama stayed busy, too jumpy to relax. She was determined to make as much fun as possible—an ice-locked holiday.

"Well, girls, how about a batch of Toll House cookies? We've got plenty of milk."

And Sara and her sisters made them eagerly, a family institution, our favorite diversionary tactic and the cure for all that ailed anyone. We used the recipe on the back of the yellow bag and stirred it by hand with a big wooden spoon. Mama didn't help; she just watched. The girls were big enough to do it. They read and measured together.

The dry ingredients came first, and then the packed brown sugar and regular sugar separately. Next they added the butter and eggs. Then all were dumped in together in the big pale-green glass mixing bowl. Shaun would start the stirring because it was hard at first. When it got easier, she gave Sara the spoon. Then Caroline stirred last when the dough was all creamy and smooth.

They ate the dough raw, one big fat fingerfull after another. Mama didn't say a word. There would be plenty to bake, and if we ran out of cookies, we'd make more.

Later in the day, Mama came and found Sara. She'd been listening to the radio.

Mama seemed really shy, almost in awe.

"I'm so proud of the way you were willing to go out in the storm to find your friend. And you found him, too, didn't you?"

Sara felt awkward; she didn't like the way Mama was acting. Mama was the boss; she was never shy.

"Thank you, Mama."

She wasn't sure what else to say, so she gave Mama a big hug.

Sara didn't want to think about our terrifying experience, much less talk about it, any more than I did. There was no way to explain.

It was best to leave those memories buried deep, deeper even than the frozen snow drifts.

Fathoms deep.

It was best to leave those memories sealed in the icy tomb that was almost mine.

Undisturbed forever.

CHAPTER 22

Back to Our Happy Life

The storm had been hell, but now we were in heaven. All normal business and daily activities were frozen until the ice thawed. The most you could do was talk on the phone. We were completely free to roam the house, relax, and play together. Our play kingdom had been restored to us, an inside kingdom for now.

We sat on the bed or downstairs by the wood fire in the den for hours. Sara read every book in the house aloud to me when I was awake to enjoy the story and to herself when I dozed comfortably in her lap. Mama said, "Make up your own stories, Sara. Your mind's as good as that author's; there's no reason you can't." But resting and reading were better right now.

We sang purr songs alone in her room, and she made up new ones, too. I purred my fine alto purr more strongly than ever. Our duet had always been important to me; now it seemed like a privilege to have such a special friend.

We could watch cartoons in the morning and other shows in the late afternoon but never soap operas in the middle of the day. Mama said they'd turn your mind to mush. It was time to do something productive. Sara thought they looked dreary anyway.

I visited my rubber bands every day while Sara watched openly; we didn't have any secrets from each other anymore. It was so fun to pick up the rug delicately, take the slender brown band out, and toss it over my head. I loved the way I could make them fly, twirling them with my paws. I politely skipped the side of the rug where the fat red one with the ink stains was stashed. Sara was still looking for the right kind to replace it.

We did addition and subtraction exercises on the pads of my paws. Before the storm I'd started to resist this in my mind. I would give Sara my fingers, but I thought I was too grown up to do math on them.

Now I turned my paws over to Sara with abandon, luxuriating in the joy of everyday things. She'd always loved the way my sheathed claw came out when she pressed gently on the pad. I loved to see her delight more than ever.

My deep terror continued to haunt me, and I was jittery for days. Since barely making it out of the pipe, I had to wonder if I was really as smart as I thought I was. I'd been too vain before and too sure I was always right.

My instincts had failed me. Sara's hadn't.

CHAPTER 23

Our Ice-Locked Holiday Continues

In the long, relaxing afternoons, Sara and her sisters played with their games, too. Sara tried to draw my portrait on Etch A Sketch and got pretty good at making the curved line of my head and back. Making the straight tail was easy. Then she got tired of it and shook it up.

Sara still had a favorite doll, and the case smelled like new plastic. New plastic was the smell of Christmas morning. The only smell Sara loved better was me.

Sara never played with Barbie. She thought her feet looked strange, all molded for high heels. How could you run on feet like that?

Another puzzlement was the little diary Shaun had gotten for Christmas. It locked with a tiny key. Sara asked Mama why Shaun would want a diary that locked.

"Maybe she's just expressing her thoughts and feelings. That's what words are for. Shaun has a right to a little privacy. Let's not bother her about it, Sara." And that was that.

Sometimes they listened to Shaun's transistor radio. It had a leather case you could carry it by with little holes in the leather. The leather smelled good, like a new pair of school shoes still in the box with paper between them.

But I was more fascinating than any of those things, a real-life friend, not a toy and certainly not a possession. When she got tired of games, Sara draped me over her shoulders like a scarf and called me the "Beauregard stole." She'd center me evenly on her neck and then let go of my hands and feet. I balanced there while she walked up and down the stairs and all over the house.

"Look, Mama. Look!"

When I finally lost my balance, I relaxed as I slid slowly and let her catch me. I never used my claws. I knew I could use them to fight an animal in the woods, if I had to. But with Sara my claws were only for counting.

Mama made one fine meal after another: meatloaf with mashed potatoes, green beans simmering all day with a ham bone, fried chicken with crispy crust and juicy meat. There was only one tablespoon of oil missing after she fried it; she measured it to show us. Then there was chicken potpie the next night. We had buttermilk cornbread baked in the big cast iron skillet where you heat the skillet in the oven first. The batter had to sizzle when you poured it in to make a nice brown crust.

There was her scrumptious pot roast, cooked so long that you could pull it in strings, with all the good gravy and little rolls to sop it up. Just sop it gently without making circles or drawing pictures on your plate.

One night we had pancakes and smoky link sausages. Mama put her hand low over the bottom of the skillet to feel how hot it was and poured the batter when it was just right. Her pancakes were golden and tender, served in stacks with Mrs. Butterworth's syrup, heated to make the butter melt.

I ate from my bowl on the floor. I didn't get table scraps, and I would never have begged at the table. How rude! I ate my own delicious canned cat food, but I feasted with them nonetheless.

Most of all, we feasted on each other's company, as nourishing as the colorful meals.

We were all stuck inside together, and it was so much fun.

CHAPTER 24

Family Fun Every Night

Some nights Mama would clear the dinner dishes and sit back down at the big, round table to tell stories, one of our very favorite treats. She was a superb storyteller—she'd learned to spin yarns growing up on her family's farm in the mountains of Chickamauga, Georgia. It was a prized form of family entertainment.

There was the tale about the panther that followed her aunt home over a mountain path one night. Her aunt never saw the panther, but she could hear it breathing, gliding close behind her. The panther never tried to get her, but they saw the big paw prints in the morning. That story was so scary it made our hair stand up on the back of our necks.

There was the one about Sara's uncles building a real log cabin in the woods down the road and towing it home on a truck. The girls played in it when they visited their grandparents. A country version of a playhouse, as sacred as the treehouse in our backyard between two pine trees overlooking the woods. It swayed in the breeze, but it never fell.

There was the fascinating story about the wandering man during the Great Depression whom Mama had fed on the back stoop when she was just a little girl. He'd said, "Little lady, do you have some food for a hungry man?" Mama had been home alone and not scared at all, only proud that she had food to share. She'd put together a fine plate for him and even given him cornbread wrapped up in cloth to take with him.

The homeless men showed up often because they had marked the house with a hobo sign down by the road. The mark meant it was a good place to be fed. Mama said it was their duty to feed the homeless men.

Once, a desperate young family had shown up. Mama lent her doll cradle to the new baby they carried in their arms.

She was proud to give it.

People in the country were so poor they would leave a burlap sack holding a litter of kittens at the end of the long driveway to the farmhouse. If Mama's family couldn't take them, they were headed for the creek to drown. But Grandmother always did, and the cats lived outside under the barn and in a hollow tree in the side yard. There were around forty of them at one point.

That's why Mama said you had to have pets "fixed."

There was the story about the little black duck that lost its mother and became Mama's pet. The little duck had shadowed Mama everywhere, all around the farmyard and throughout their property.

And he visited on the front porch too, just like the rest of the family.

But our very favorite story was about Mama's beloved little dog, Buster. Mama had Buster when she was older, during high school and then her college years at the University of Georgia. She used to come home from college on the Greyhound bus once a semester, which was as often as they could afford the bus ticket.

Grandmother would start prepping Buster a week before Mama was set to arrive. "She'll be home in seven days, Buster." The little dog's eyes would light up. Then, "She'll be getting off the Greyhound bus in six days, Buster." And on throughout the week.

On the day Mama was scheduled to arrive, Grandmother would say, "She'll be home today, Buster."

And Buster would trot down the half-mile dirt driveway and sit by the side of the road, eager with anticipation. He'd wait patiently for hours as the cars went by. None of those held Mama.

But when the big, smelly bus ground to a halt and opened its doors, he was there, ready to welcome Mama home from college and escort her proudly up to the house. They both jumped for joy on the way.

Mama loved Buster.

CHAPTER 25

Rainbows Inside and Out

The blissful snow days continued to unfold. After a few days, some of the parents on our street walked a mile up the hill to the nearest convenience store, pulling sleds. They loaded up and came back home with fresh milk and other supplies.

We baked another batch of cookies. Our milk supply had been renewed.

Sara and I ran up and down the stairs as fast as we could, two at a time, and Sara slid down the curved banister when Mama wasn't looking. I could run down it fast without losing my footing, even though it was slick.

Sometimes Sara suggested a game of hide-and-seek, but I only pretended to play.

My hiding days were over.

And often we just lay together in the bright sunshine that beamed in the big windows, reflecting off the ice-sculptured world outside. Sara saw rainbows on the windowsill.

But then Sara saw rainbows everywhere. In the summer she'd see a rainbow in a puddle on the street where a drop of gasoline had spilled.

Of course, the best rainbows were the tiny ones Sara saw in my fur. She counted them again and again. Then she'd tickle me under my armpits, and I'd stretch out longer and longer, spreading my fingers and toes and reaching.

This was the happiest time of all.

I was a sultan once again, but a sultan who had learned not to hide.

It took a long time before the plows made it to our street.

Sara and her sisters were out of school for an entire week. And there was no bus stop duty for me. So I was out of school, too.

CHAPTER 26

My Friend, My Treasure

Every night Sara and I would go up to our room and climb into bed together. She sat up for a long time, giving me a butterfly kiss and an Eskimo kiss for extra and then rubbing me and singing purr songs until she was too tired. The Kit-Cat clock ticktocked assertively, and Sara's heart beat the quiet "lub dub" that made me feel all was right with the world.

I'd close my eyes and lay awake marveling that I was here at all, grateful with every millimeter of my being, from the tip of my nose to the tip of my tail and every tiny rainbow in between.

Mama had made the call that saved my life, bowing to the sheer sincerity of Sara's conviction that she must look for me.

Mama never looked back. Nor did she apologize.

In her own way, she had been the most courageous of us all.

The neighbors criticized Mama. They said that letting Sara go out in the storm to search for me had been "against all reason."

But I will ask you this: What did "reason" ever have to do with love?

Or with miracles?

If I'd looked into the future, I'd have seen that it was the only time in her life Sara ever crossed wills with Mama and won.

But I was too busy wringing all the joy out of every minute to worry about the future. I didn't have nine lives, only this one.

And I'd spend it snuggled up against my little girl, safe and warm and content, ready to rest for the night and then get up and cherish another happy day with my family.

One day as exultant as the next.

She was one of life's rarest treasures, Sara was. A friend willing to make a sacrifice for you.

"Lub dub, lub dub, ticktock."

"Meh-eh, Beauregard. I love you. Good night."

"Meh-eh, Sara. I love you too."

It was the coziest the red-gingham bed had ever been.

Maureen O'Rourke Woods holds a degree in English and a master's in mass communications. She is now retired from a successful twenty-five-year career as a creative director and award-winning copywriter of health-care advertising and marketing. A dedicated advocate at her local shelter, she played an active role in securing county funding for a new shelter facility. She intends to use proceeds from *Beauregard and the Blizzard* to fund programs for homeless pets throughout her home state of South Carolina. Woods and her husband are parents to three rescue pets: Tuxedo cats Scout and Leonardo, and American Eskimo/mix Shadow.

Ablast of Arctic air collided with a Gulf Coast storm to create the weather system in this story, now known as the Blizzard of 1966. It traveled up the Atlantic Seaboard on Saturday, January 29, packing gale-force winds clocked at fifty-four miles per hour and temperatures in the low teens. The wind blew out plate-glass windows and whipped snowdrifts up to twelve feet high.

The blizzard paralyzed the Washington, DC, area, dumping up to sixteen inches of snow on top of the six inches already on the ground.[1]

The nation's capital shut down completely; roads were impassable, and Dulles Airport and

Union Station closed. Military helicopters, police, and radio stations worked together to perform emergency rescues, transporting doctors to seriously ill patients and mothers giving birth to hospitals.[3]

Nationwide, 142 people died due to the massive storm.[4]

Beauregard didn't.

To see a newsreel about the Blizzard of 1966, go to

https://www.youtube.com/watch?v=tijtM0qoHtM.

ENDNOTES

1. Kevin Ambrose, Dan Henry, and Andy Weiss, "Winter Storms and Blizzards," in *Washington Weather: The Weather Sourcebook for the D.C. Area* (Historical Enterprises, 2002), 76–79.

2. National Centers for Environmental Information, "The Northeast Snowfall Impact Scale," accessed November 3, 2017, https://www.ncdc.noaa.gov/snow-and-ice/rsi/nesis.

3. Universal Newsreel, "B-R-R-R! Blizzard Flays Atlantic Coast," filmed January 1966, YouTube video, 1:54, posted by "PublicDomainFootage. com," posted on January 30, 2011, Accessed

November 21, 2017. https://www.youtube.com/watch?v=tijtM0qoHtM.

4. "Blizzard's Death Toll Mounts to 142," *Morning Herald* (Hagerstown, MD), February 2, 1966, 1.

Made in the USA
Columbia, SC
12 November 2022